The Parable of
The Sower

Nico Baalbergen

ISBN: 978-1-78364-584-8

The Open Bible Trust

www.obt.org.uk

Quotations from the Bible are mainly from the *New International Version* with some from the *New English Bible* and others being the author's own translation.

****

THE OPEN BIBLE TRUST
Fordland Mount, Upper Basildon,
Reading, RG8 8LU, UK

The Parable of The Sower

Contents

Page

Preface

The kingdom of God is a popular topic, but there is much confusion as to its exact meaning, since it appears to be used in so many different ways. The present booklet starts from the assumption that it is the kingdom of God, and that it cannot possibly be understood apart from God's sovereignty intervening in the affairs of man. No human effort can help in bringing about his kingdom.

It is, of course, not claimed that the interpretation offered in this booklet is the only one possible. With his present light and understanding, it is one which appears to the author to make sense and to agree best with the context in which it was spoken.

In order to follow this study, the reader will need to have some degree of familiarity with the three forms in which this parable is found in the Gospels. This can be gained by the simple expedient of careful reading, therefore the complete text is given on the next pages. It is printed in three parallel columns, showing clearly where the three evangelists agree and where they have different wordings.

The English version used was mainly NIV, sometimes compared with NEB and KJV, and sometimes corrected to agree better with the Greek original.

It is the author's hope and prayer that by this little booklet the reader may come to a deeper understanding of the word and, above all, grow in the knowledge and love of the Lord Jesus Christ, our Saviour.

The Parable of the Sower

Matthew 13:1-23	Mark 4:1-20	Luke 8:4-15
1. The same day Jesus went out of the house and sat by the sea. 2. Such large crowds gathered around Him that He got into a boat and sat down, while all the people stood on the shore.	1. And again He began to teach by the sea. The crowd that gathered around him was so large that He got into a boat and sat down on the sea, while all the people were on the shore by the sea. 2. He taught them many things in parables, and said in His teaching:	4. While a large crowd was gathering and people were coming to Jesus from town to town, He told this parable:
3.Then He told them many things in parables, saying: "Look, He has gone out, the sower to sow.	3. Listen! Look, he has gone out, the sower, to sow.	5. "He has gone out, the sower, to sow his seed.
4. As he was sowing, some seeds fell along the path, and the birds came and ate them up.	4.As he was sowing, some seeds fell along the path, and the birds came and ate it up.	As he was sowing, some seed fell along the path; it was trampled on, and the birds of the air ate it up.
5. Some seeds fell on rocky places, where they did not have much soil. They sprang up quickly, because the soil was shallow. 6. But when the sun came up, the (plants) were scorched, and they withered, because they had no root.	5. Some seeds fell on rocky places, it did not have much soil. It sprang up quickly, because the soil was shallow. 6. But when the sun came up, the (plants) were scorched, and they withered because they had no root.	6. Some seed fell on rock, and when it came up, the (plants) withered because they had no moisture.

7. Other seeds fell on the thorns which grew up and choked the (plants).	7. Other seed fell into the thorns, which grew up and choked the (plants) so that they did not bear grain.	7. Other seed fell among thorns, which grew up with it and choked the (plants).
8. But other seeds fell on good soil, where they produced a crop – a hundred, sixty and thirty times what was sown. He who has ears, let him hear".	8. But (all the) other seeds fell into the good soil, where they produced a crop when they grew up and increased, and bore thirty, sixty and a hundred times what was sown". 9. Then Jesus said: "Who has ears to hear, let him hear". 10. When He was alone, those around Him and the twelve asked Him about parables. 11. He told them, "To you has been given the secret of the Kingdom of God, but to those on the outside all these things come in parables,	8. And other seed fell into the good soil. Having grown up it produced a crop, a hundred times more than was sown". When He said this, He called out: "He who has ears to hear, let him hear". 9. His disciples asked Him what this parable meant.
10. The disciples came to him and asked, "Why do You speak to the people in parables?" 11. He replied, "because to you has been given to know the secrets of the kingdom of the heavens, but to them it is not given. 12. For who ever has will be given more, and he will have an abundance; but whoever does not have, even what he has will be taken from him. 13. This is why I speak to them in parables, because seeing they do not see; and hearing they do not understand.		10. He said, "To you has been given to know the secrets of the kingdom of God, but to others
	12. so that, seeing they will see but not perceive, and hearing they will hear but not understand; lest they turn (to God) and be forgiven!".	(I speak) in parables so that, though seeing, they will not see; and hearing they will not understand.

14. In them is fulfilled the prophecy of Isaiah: You will hear but not understand at all; and you will see but not perceive at all.		
15. For this people's heart has become calloused; and with their ears they hardly hear, and their eyes they have closed, lest they see with their eyes, and their ears hear, and with their hearts understand and turn, and I shall heal them. 16. But blessed are your eyes because they see, and your ears because they hear. 17. For I tell you the truth, many prophets and righteous men longed to see what you see but did not see it, and to hear what you hear but did not hear it.	13. Then Jesus said to them: "Don't you understand this parable? How then will you understand any parable?"	
18. Listen to what the parable of the sower means.	14. The sower sows the seed.	11. This is the meaning of the parable: The seed is the word of God.
19. When anyone hears the message about the kingdom and does not understand it, the evil one comes and snatches away what was sown in his heart. This is the seed sown along the path.	15. Some people are like the seed along the path, where the word is sown. As soon as they hear it, Satan comes and takes away the word that was sown in them.	12. Those along the path are the ones who hear, the devil comes and takes away the word from their hearts, so that they may not believe and be saved.

20. The one who received the seed that fell on rocky places is the man who hears the word and at once receives it with joy.	16. Others, like seed sown on rocky places, hear the word and at once receive it with joy.	13. Those on the rock are the ones who receive the word with joy when they hear it, but they have no root.
21. But since he has not root in himself, he lasts only a short time. When trouble or persecution comes because of the word, he quickly stumbles and falls.	17. But since they have no root in themselves, they last only a short time. When trouble or persecution comes because of the word, they quickly stumble and fall.	They believe for a while, but in the time of testing they fall away.
22. The one who received the seed that fell among the thorns is the man who hears the word, but the worries of this age and the deceitfulness of wealth choke it, making it unfruitful.	18. Still others like the seed sown among thorns, hear the word: 19. But worries of this age, the deceitfulness of wealth and the desires for other things come in and choke the word, making it unfruitful.	14. That which fell in the midst of the thorns stands for those who hear, but as they go on their way they are choked by life's worries, riches and pleasures, and they do not bear (fruit) to maturity.
23. But the one who received the seed that fell in the good soil is the man who hears the word and understands it. He produces a crop, yielding a hundred, sixty or thirty times what was sown".	20. And all those others, like the seed sown in the good soil, hear the word, accept it, and produce a crop – thirty, sixty or even a hundred times what was sown."	15. But the seed in the good soil stands for those with a noble and good heart who hear the word, retain it, and by perseverance, produce a crop."

Introduction

During His earthly ministry our Lord taught the people many things by way of parables. Outstanding among them is that "of the Sower". It is told by both Matthew (13:1-23) and Mark (4:1-20) as well as by Luke (8:4-15). It can hardly be accidental that the parables are recorded in the order in which we have them. This parable of the sower stands more or less on its own and seems to be intended as a key to understanding the other parables, the more so as Christ Himself insisted: "You do not understand this parable? How then are you to understand any parable?" (Mark 4:13). Thus it appears that a proper understanding of this particular parable is basic and fundamental to an understanding of the other parables spoken by the Lord. This view is strengthened by the position given to this parable in the three Gospels and again by the fact that it is accompanied by an interpretation of its meaning.

The three evangelists differ in their arrangement of the events leading up to and following the story of the parable. Nevertheless, it seems clear that it marks something of a turning point in the ministry and teaching of the Lord Jesus Christ. Large crowds were gathering around Him and He was becoming quite popular as a preacher and healer. At the same time there was severe criticism and doubt. All three evangelists relate how the Pharisees reproached Him for allowing His disciples to pick ears of corn on the Sabbath, and in both Matthew and Mark they accuse Him of being an agent of Beelzebub, the prince of demons, in driving out demons. But even His relatives and friends misunderstood Him, as reported by all three evangelists (Matthew 12:46-50 and Mark 2:31-35), although Luke holds this incident over to 8:19-21. This is the situation in which the Lord had to work and so He introduced a new phase in His teaching. Just as in Mark 3:7, where He moved away from those who had become His enemies, so here He deliberately turns His back on His human kith and kin. It is Mark alone who gives explicit expression to this point by opening this new development with the words *kai palin,* and again, *"a second time".*

It is true that in His mission in a fallen world, the Lord has to reckon with rocky soil, well-trodden paths, thistles, birds and scorching heat. But "we should also note that the fact that the world is made and sustained by God and that the word of promise partakes of his omnipotence dictating that these harsh realities will never amount to more than the *context* in which the work of grace operates" (Beasley-Murray, *Jesus,* p.130). In spite of all the hindrances that prevent the seed from coming to fruition, the word (Matthew *Of the Kingdom*, Mark *of God,* Luke) continues to do its work and does not return empty and so "God brings forth the triumphant end which He had promised" (Jeremias, *Parables,* p.150). It seems odd that some commentators think that the so-called four-fold sowing should mean that three-quarters of the seed was to be wasted and lost, over against only one-quarter bearing fruit. Rather that with a four-fold description of the fate of the seeds the parable presents us with "a formal balance and contrast between three situations of waste and failure and three situations of gain and success" (Crossan, *In Parables*, p.41; quoted in Beasley-Murray, *Jesus*, p.128). "The general sense of the parable is not that the fate of the seed depends on the nature of the soil, but the fact that the sower can get an extremely rich harvest" (Dahl, *"The Parables of Growth",* quoted in Beasley-Murray, *Jesus*, p.129). This would mean that the Parable of the Sower is less a picture of God's kingdom struggling against all sorts of unfavorable conditions and influences that as expression of divine assurance that God's saving rule and sovereignty, notwithstanding opposition and misunderstanding, will break through in our human condition bringing a fullness of blessings.

After these introductory remarks we shall now consider the parable itself as well as its interpretation as given by the Lord. In all three gospels the interpretation is separated from the actual story by a discussion of the purpose the Lord had in telling parables. This section will also receive our attention.

The setting

The Parable of the Sower is told by the Lord during His ministry in Galilee. And so, we see Him here near the Lake of Galilee, also known as Lake Kinnereth.

In chapter thirteen Matthew groups together eight parables, and also gives an explanation of the reason why the Lord was using this particular form of teaching. The whole section from 12:15 to 13:52 is visualized between two attendances at synagogue and so may be a condensation of one week's ministry of the Lord. After His mother and brothers had come wanting to see Him, "that same day" He went out of the house, probably at Capernaum (Matthew 4:13; 9:1), situated on the coast of the lake. Thus we find a contrast in continuity. It seems as if Matthew wants to show that His breach with them does in no way mean that He discontinues His teaching of the crowds. And so chronologically this section is connected with the foregoing. Mark is more emphatic in stressing a new beginning, as already remarked above. Luke, on the other hand, is far less specific as to time and place. In 18:1 he tells of the Lord's travelling ministry from town to town, and then, in verse 4, goes on describing the people that come to hear Him. All the same, by recording only this one parable, he indeed manages to rivet our attention on it, thus giving it even more prominence than the other two evangelists.

Luke does not mention either ship or lake, but both Matthew and Mark lay stress on the fact that the crowd of people gathering around the Lord was so large that He sought His refuge in a boat, just as He had done on another occasion (Mk 3:9) to avoid being crushed by the people, or from being pushed into the water. In the boat He sits down, the usual posture for a teacher (comp. Luke 4:20; 10:39; Acts 22:3). See also Luke 5:3: "Then he sat down and taught the people from the boat."

In the following sentence the evangelists continue to stress this picture of a Teacher, indicating at the same time His particular mode of teaching. "To tell", or "to say", in this context comes near to being an equivalent of "to teach" as can be amply illustrated from Rabbinical usage ("*omer*", "said Rabbi So and So"). Matthew and Mark record that Christ taught in (the form of) parables. Luke says the same thing when he uses the singular without the article. This does not necessarily mean, as some commentators would have it, that only one parable is to follow. The singular without the article is often used to indicate character or nature. So Luke tells us about the characteristic manner of the Lord's teaching: "through parables", "by way of parable".

Parables are pictures of familiar scenes or events drawn from the experiences of everyday life. These pictures are not just used as illustrations of some point in the teaching, they are connected with spiritual realities. In the past the parables have often been explained as if they were allegories, but there are many points of difference between an allegory and a parable. An allegory is a totally imaginary story and is composed in such a way that every detail in it is used as a symbol for something quite different. A famous example of this sort of story is the *Pilgrim's Progress*. A parable is not so made up. It is a scene or event drawn from real life, such as we may expect to come across at any time. Usually it has only one single point of comparison and most of the details play a role in the realism of the picture and serve to strengthen its credibility, but are not meant to have a special significance of their own. And so a parable is more of a "riddle" in which the pictorial part is more or less the outside. The hearer must look through this pictorial part as if through a window and try to see the truth of higher order which shines through. After the pictorial part has been told, it is then left to the hearer ("disciple") to find and understand the meaning and substance of the parable. A parable, therefore, demands mental exertion from the hearer and leaves it entirely up to him to fathom the correct interpretation. The reason for this use of parables is that the natural life and the spiritual life have so much affinity. Both "form a grand unity in their relation to the Living God Who reigneth" (A. Edersheim, *Life and Times of Jesus the Messiah,* page 582). Christ did not need to make up illustrations for the truths He was teaching. "He found them ready-made by the Maker of man and nature" (Dodd, *Parables*, page 20).

The Parable of the Sower

In Mark the parable begins with the appeal: "Hear, Listen!". With the call of 4:9 it forms an *inclusion* (or doubling up) under the word "to hear", as in Mark 7:14-16. "When this figure is used, it marks what is said as being comprised in one complete circle, thus calling our attention to its solemnity; giving completeness of the statement that is made, or to the truth enumerated, thus making and emphasizing its importance". (Further on this literary figure in E.W. Bullinger, *Figures of Speech in the Bible* [1898], Reprint Baker, Grand Rapids, 1971, pp.245-249.).

Most important among the Old Testament invitations to hear became the one which introduced the daily recitation of the "Hear O Israel" (Dt. 6:4). In New Testament times this was already in common usage among devout Jews. "To hear" in the sense of "to learn a tradition" is much older than its use in the rabbinical literature. In the Old Testament "to hear" (*shemah*) may have this shade of meaning. Isaiah 28:23-29 is a beautiful example of didactic style. It deals with the complicated and meaningful activities of the farmer in sowing and harvesting. The section opens with an invitation to hear and pay particular attention to what is going to be taught: "Listen and hear what I say." In Deuteronomy, with its special interest in teaching, this sort of introduction is frequent, e.g. 4:1; 5:1; 6:4; 9:1; 27:9; 32:1. And even more so in the so-called wisdom literature e.g. Proverbs 1:8; 4:1,10; 5:7; 7:24; 8:32,33; 23:19,22; 28:9 Psalms 34:11. The prophets, too, lay stress on "hearing", e.g. Isaiah 1;10; 46:3,12; 551:1,4,7; 55:3; Jeremiah

9:20; Joel 1:2, Micah 6:1,9; Particularly telling in this connection is Isaiah 50:4,5:

> "He awakens me morning by morning"
> wakens my ear like one being taught
> The Sovereign Lord has opened my ears,
> and I have not been rebellious:
> I have not drawn back."

In the Talmud this introduction becomes extremely frequent; "Come and hear", so much so that for the ancient sages of Israel the verb "to hear" describes the real and proper activity of the *talmid*, the "disciple", and means to appropriate to oneself the teaching of the master by careful and exact listening. W. Bacher, *Die exegetishe Terminologie der Judischen Traditionsliteratur,* vol.1, p.189; vol.II,p. 219.

So when His contemporaries heard Christ's call "to listen", two thoughts in particular would spring to mind: (1) Somebody wants to utter a particular word claiming authority. So he uses an invitation that was used in such "holy scriptures" as the "Hear Israel" and in the teaching of the prophets; (2) Here speaks a teacher whose aim is that his words should be taken to heart and learnt.

After thus opening the parable with the appeal to listen, the Lord rounds it off with" He who has ears to listen, let him listen: to emphasize that He is not just telling an interesting story, but is about to give a revelation of some aspect of His Messianic mission.

In the Greek "the Sower" has the article. Most of the translations treat this as generic, translating it "a" sower, as if the Lord is speaking of just any sower, but this seems rather out of tune with the whole setting the evangelists give to this parable, and to the interpretation given it by the Lord. It would seem to be more in line to keep the definite article and write the Sower with a capital letter, suggesting that the Lord refers to Himself.

In the land of Israel the time of sowing is entirely dependent on the coming of the "early rains". After the long and dry summer the soil is parched and dusty and totally unfit for sowing. Towards the end of October, the anxiously awaited heavy rains begin to fall. This opens the agricultural year. The hard and cracked soil is softened and the farmer begins plowing, using the old plow, not the heavy implement we are more or less familiar with. It was a wooden stake with a metal tip (the plow point) at the bottom, which had to be sharpened every so often. The ground could not be turned over as is done by our modern plows. The farmer tried to loosen the soil to a sufficient depth and sometimes had to go over the field more than once; then followed the sowing. The seed is sown broadcast and not in furrows. Afterwards it was either plowed in or raked by means of a branch or a bush which was dragged over the ground. Harrowing proper seems not to have been known. Sowing by hand was preferably done in the early morning (Ecclesiastes 11:4-6) when there was no wind blowing and the ground was still moist. The industrious farmer was fully occupied in plowing and sowing before the heavy winter rains might make it impossible for him to do his work. Thus, he hoped for a rich harvest as a crown on his labor. A lazy man allowed the right time to pass by and had nothing to show when harvest time came (Proverbs 20:4).

The "early rains" may be late and then the farmer can only wait till the rains come to refresh the thirsty soil. Till the end of November, the rainfall is not large. From December to February is the period of heavy rainfalls. The "latter rains" are the heavy showers of March and April. Coming before the harvest and the summer drought, they are of more importance to the country than the rains of winter; the grain must ripen; a good harvest is to a large extent dependent on this "latter rain". That is why it is so important that the rains come at *the proper time* (Deuteronomy 11:14; Jeremiah 5:24).

So "the Sower went out to sow (His seed)". The amazing thing is that many commentators seem to think that this particular sower was one who went to cast away and waste three-quarters of his seed before sowing only one-quarter in the good and well-prepared part of his field. But is this the picture the Lord is painting? What farmer would be willing to waste so much of his costly seed? Even though we have a complex picture set before us in this parable, the importance of the *harvest* should not be denied (cf. Beasley-Murray, *Jesus*, p. 128 f).

Although there are situations of waste and failure, the harvest is of truly exceptional size. Mark gives the answer. In 4:8 he does not say "and other seed", putting this seed that fell on good soil on a level with the three parts that were wasted. He uses the singular for the first three sowings, but the plural for the fourth and large sowing in the good soil: "some (*ho men*) fell along the path ...some other (*allo*) fell on rocky places ... some (*allo*) fell among thorns ...and (*all the*) other seeds (*alla,* plural) fell into the good soil," emphasizing that most of the seed was sown where it should have been sown.

Luke adds the seemingly redundant object "his seed", thus making it clear that the parable reaches up to something more; the seed is the word of God spoken by the Lord (cf. 2 Corinthians 9:10).

When sowing broadcast by hand it cannot be avoided that some seeds fall along and even on the road. It is difficult to see how some commentators think that this road was going through the plowed field. Even if a path across the field was made in summer, unlikely as this seems, after the preparatory plowing it would have disappeared. It would seem more likely to be the regular path or roadway alongside the field. Luke confirms this by saying: "(the seed) was trampled on (trodden down, A.V.)." Seed scattered in the verge of a path and possibly even on the path itself, does not find any soft earth to sink into, so it gets trampled on. "And the birds came and ate it up". And that, unfortunately, was the end of those seeds.

The rocky places are not places strewn with rocks or stones. In some places the earth is not deep because the rock of the subsoil crops out, coming up near to the surface. The earth there forms only a thin layer without much depth. Roots cannot grow deep to form a system, and neither will the earth be able to hold moisture. Yet it is not unusual for seeds to germinate quickly in such a shallow place. Before they have the opportunity of growing a system of roots, however, the hot sun will draw off the little moisture the earth may have held, and the tender plants will wither fast because of lack of roots. Here again some good seeds are lost to the farmer.

Thistles are a very persistent weed. Even if the plants are dead after the long and hot summer, their seeds are waiting for the rains to sprout again. When the ground was cursed because of the sin of Adam (Genesis 3:17,18), one of the results was to be that it would produce thorns and thistles for man. Some of the seeds the sower was casting fell where thistles may already have begun to grow. NEB very graphically translates: "the thistles shot up." In comparison with the wheat they grow much faster and by their luxurious growth manage to choke the wheat. Even though it might have shown some promise and possibly have produced ears, the wheat had no possibility of maturing and bringing a crop to completion.

We now come to the main part and the thrust of the parable. "We can almost picture to ourselves the Saviour seated in the prow of the boat as He points His hearers to the rich plains over against Him, where the young corn, still in the first green of its growing, is giving promise of harvest" (Edersheim, *The Life and Times of Jesus,* part 1, p. 586). Most of the seed has fallen on and into the good earth. This "good" earth cannot be anything else but the ordinary, cultivated and fertile soil. This was much more than a fourth part of the farmer's field. The Master Storyteller did not make an insipid comparison of four different kinds of soil, leaving it to the hearers to make their choice. It is a well-composed story beginning with minor, although important, details, and building up towards a climax. The point stressed in the story comes at the end. True, there are all sorts of obstacles the seed is encountering. But the seed is good and the soil is good and so these two combine in producing fruit. "And the seed having sprouted produced fruit, having grown up and increased, and yielded up to a hundred times what was sown."

It is remarkable that the story stops short here and does not go on to speak of the actual harvest time. Let us heed the words of the Lord: "Consider carefully how you listen and what you hear" (Luke 8:18; Mark 4:24). Other parables do refer to the reaping, but not this one. The meaning of this will be further considered when we shall discuss the interpretation the Lord Himself gave of this parable. What strikes us here is the unexpectedly large yield the seed gives. Often reference is made to the harvest Isaac reaped (Genesis 26). When there was famine in the land, Isaac went to Abimelech, king of the Philistines in Gerar. The Lord did not allow

Isaac to go down to Egypt, because that was not the land that the Lord was to give to him and his descendants. And then in verse 12: "Isaac planted crops in that land and that same year reaped a hundredfold, because the Lord blessed him." Note well that this was in a context of a year of famine! Later on the Lord gave this promise to the children of Israel: "Worship the Lord your God, and His blessing will be on your food and water" (Exodus 23:25).

We have no Biblical facts as to the possible yield of wheat or barley. In our days we are accustomed to high yields and this will easily give us wrong ideas about the production in Israel. The amount of sowing-seed used is dependent on several things, such as size of the seed, time of sowing, type of soil and manuring. In the years before the last war yield would be from twenty to twenty-five times the amount of seed used, at least in "normal" years. In the sixties this was about thirty times, showing that productivity has increased. Apart from climate and type of soil, yield in the land of Israel will have been much lower. Possibly the situation can best be compared with that of Europe some centuries ago. Historical research has shown that in the ninth century the yield for wheat and barley was from 2.5 to 3 on some farms in the North of France. In England this was from 4 to 5 in the thirteenth century. Even in the 18th. century, yield often was no higher than from about four to five times the amount of seed used. If we assume that in Israel in normal years yield was about five times the amount of seed used, we may conclude that the farmer could expect to reap five bushels of wheat for every bushel sown. One bushel had to be reserved for sowing for the new season and four remained for consumption. If the farmer had a bad year and reaped only three bushels for the own sown, he simply had not enough left for his own consumption. This could lead to borrowing with all its adverse consequences. So we see that Isaac's harvest was far beyond the normal expectation.

Sometimes it is thought that the summing up of the yield in the parable of the Sower indicated the different sorts of believers, but this seems unlikely. Once again it should be stressed that not all details are to be decoded. Moreover, a safeguard seems to be built in by the variations as given by the three evangelists. Matthew finishes with an anticlimax: from a hundred to sixty to thirty. Mark has a climax, climbing from thirty to sixty to a hundred, and Luke has simply a hundred-fold yield. The most probable interpretation seems to be that we have to think of the blessings in the Messianic Age. In Psalms 67:6 we read: "Then the land will yield its harvest, and God, our God, will bless us." Hosea refers to this (2:20-22): "… and the earth will respond to the grain …", as does Jeremiah 31:27f. and Isaiah 55:10f. In the rebirth of the Nation not only will mankind receive countless blessings, but nature too.

The parable is ended, but before concluding His address, the Lord "cries out" (Luke an emphatic word), "He who has ears, let him hear!" In his gospel John records three times (7:28,37; 12:44) that the Lord proclaims something in a loud voice. The same is said of John the Baptist in 1:15, clearly an important prophetic announcement. This may well indicate that the emphasis with which the words are spoken in a loud voice aim at directing the attention of the hearers to the words taught, telling them that they should be taken to heart and memorized.

Since, as remarked before, Mark began the parable with the appeal to listen, this conclusion gives added emphasis to the importance and urgency of what is being taught. "Jesus's teaching is not the leisurely and patient exposition of a system by the founder of a school. It is related to a brief and tremendous crisis in which He is the principal figure and which indeed His appearance brought about" (Dodd, *Parables*, p.23). More is at stake in this parable than seems apparent at first sight. It is all a matter of hearing, or rather, listening; that difficult and mysterious connection between hearing and listening. Neither Greek nor Hebrew use different verbs for this distinction. In Matthew 15:10 and Mark 7:14 the verb "to understand" is added to "listening" to make this distinction explicit. Many are the people who listen without hearing anything, or hear without listening. To understand the meaning of the parable and to make the correct application requires opened ears, so that the Word of God is heard, which has the power to save (Ezekiel 3:27).

The reason for speaking in parables

Between the parable and its interpretation, a difficult and much-debated passage about the purpose of this method of teaching in parables is inserted. That it is inserted here shows the importance to be attached to it. It forms, as it were, the center piece of the section as a whole.

After the parable is told there is a sudden shift in scene. The crowds are fading out of the picture and the Lord is alone with his disciples and other close followers, the Holy Spirit guiding us to think about the meaning of what is being recorded.

The parable of the sower may look deceptively simple once the interpretation is given, yet the disciples deemed it necessary to ask about its meaning. Matthew tells us that they even inquired about this specific form of teaching. Apparently they were puzzled. The method remained a burden to them and it is almost with a sigh of relief that they say much later: "Now You are speaking in plain language and do not pose a riddle" (John 16:29). But then, the parables are used to induce the hearers to be careful in their listening and to exercise all their thinking powers to make the correct application. For those who have chosen to do God's will, the difficulties can be solved (cf. John 7:17).

While Luke says only that the disciples asked about the meaning of this particular parable, Mark adds that the Lord was "on His own" and tells others beside the twelve. The disciples' questioning is answered in two parts. Before giving the interpretation of the parable, the Lord enlightens His disciples about the reason for teaching in parables.

The Lord's answer begins with an emphatically placed "to you" in order to make a contrast with what follows. The verb is given in the perfect passive tense, which is a circumlocution of the Divine action and should be taken as meaning "God has given". Thus, once again, stress is laid on the fact that understanding does not come by human reasoning, but that it is a revelation given by God (cf. Matthew16:17; John 3:27).

At the same time the Lord accentuates the privileged position into which His friends and disciples have come. They find themselves in a situation more or less comparable to that of Abraham (Genesis 18:17): Then the Lord said: "Shall I hide from Abraham what I am about to do?" Later on the Lord Himself declares (John 15:15): "I have called you friends, for everything I learned from My Father I have told you." God has given to them the secrets of the Kingdom of God. Matthew And Luke Both add this verb "to know", thus making it explicit what Mark leaves unsaid; for to be given a secret really means to know about it. The secrets here relate to the Kingdom of God (Matthew, of the Heavens). It does not concern complete information, but a particular piece, or pieces, of information. The situation in which the Lord finds Himself, one of response which is in part favorable and in part unfavorable with its moments of outright opposition, is one asking for added insights into this rather unexpected aspect of the manifestation of the Kingdom of God. Even John the Baptist, who had given such a clear witness concerning Christ (John 3:22-36), found himself forced to send his disciples to ask Him whether he really was the One Who was to come (Matthew 11:2-6; Luke 7:18-23). And so, under the form of parables, He reveals some aspects of the Kingdom of God which so far had remained undisclosed secrets. The Greek word for "secret", *musterion*, is frequent in Paul's letters, but in the Gospels it is only used in this connection, closely attached to the parable of the Sower. The OT back-ground for the use of this word in Daniel 2, where it occurs no fewer than eight times. In the dream and its interpretation by Daniel, the Lord God reveals how His purpose of universal rule will be realized. Here again it is clearly declared by Daniel: "No wise man, enchanter, magician or diviner can explain to the king the secret he has asked about, but there is a God in heaven Who revels secrets. He has shown king Nebuchadnezzar what will happen in days to come." In face of the doubts and the misunderstandings with regard to His mission, the Lord makes it clear to His disciples that "the word that goes out from God, will not return empty, but will accomplish what He desires: (see Isaiah 55:10-11).

The contrast is then given: to "them", to "the others", it has not been given. Luke's phrase (*toipos*, "other", "remaining") is sometimes used of non-disciples and non-believers, Acts 5:13; Romans 11:8; Ephesians 2:3; 1 Thessalonians 4:13; 5:6.) Mark's particular phrase ("those on the outside") is used in the same sense for "outsiders", people who do not belong to the group in view (1 Corinthians 5:12; Colossians. 4:5; 1 Thessalonians 4:12; 1 Timothy 3:7), and may be most naturally taken as indicating "the multitude" in general, in opposition to the intimate circle of friends and disciples of Christ.

"To those not of your number everything comes in parables." The contrasting parallelism of the two clauses in Mark 11:11 suggests that "secret" and "parable" may correspond in meaning. The word "parable" would then have the meaning of its Hebrew and Aramaic equivalents, *mashal* and *mithla*, "enigma", "riddle", "dark saying". The word "parable" is nothing but a transcription of

The Parable of the Sower   31

the Greek word *parabole*, which often is a good practice, because it forces the reader to form a proper idea as to its meaning. Unfortunately, the word has come to have a history in the many centuries of Christianity, so most people use it without any further thought. In Mark 7:17 we find the word "parable" in most translations, but it no doubt has the meaning of "dark saying", "riddle". Of Moses it was said, "with him I speak face to face, clearly and not in riddles". And the reason is given: "He is faithful in all My house." But to other prophets God was to reveal Himself in dreams and visions (Numbers 12:6,7).

To "the others", "everything comes in parables". Surprise has often been expressed about the use of "to come" (Greek *ginetai*), as this seems a strange expression to describe teaching. True, it is not idiomatic Greek, but the problem will disappear if it is realized that at the back is a very common expression in the OT. The clause, as it stands, finds an almost perfect parallel in Genesis 15:1, "The word of the Lord came to Abram in a vision." From then on the phrase is used when God speaks, for instance, to Samuel (1 Samuel 15:10), to Elijah (2 Kings 17:2,8, etc.) and frequently in the prophets. In Mark the subject of the verb "to come" is *ta panta*, "all these things", so the meaning evidently is that the Word of God embodied in the Lord Jesus Christ, that is to say the whole of His earthly ministry, whether preaching, teaching or healing comes to the multitude in general, not clearly and unequivocally, but in a veiled form. And so, all that the Lord does and says remains an enigma to those whose eyes have not been opened to the true significance of His mission. At this point in the argument Matthew (13:12) introduces the proverb: "To whoever has will be given more and he will have an abundance, but whoever does not have, even that he has will be taken from him." Both Mark (4:15) and Luke (8:18) add this later in close connection with the parable of the lamp. Moreover, they have it preceded by a renewed admonition to hear" "Consider carefully what you hear (Mark) and how you hear (Luke)." Divine teaching is not content to utter general truisms, neither is it reserved for some privileged or "educated" people.

The prophet Isaiah and the New Testament

Matthew alone then goes on to quote in full the words of the commission given to Isaiah (6:9-10), not as given in the Hebrew text, but according to the Greek translation of the Septuagint. This is all the more important, since this passage is quoted in exactly the same words by the Apostle Paul in Acts 28:26-27.

In the long list of quotations from the Old Testament in the New, after the book of Psalms, Isaiah is the book most often quoted, and accounts for about 14% of all quotations. This alone should make us pause and think.

The prophet's name Isaiah stands for the Hebrew name *Yeshayah*, or rather in the longer form *Yeshayahu*, meaning "The Lord saves", "The Lord is salvation", or "Salvation of The Lord". He is the Great Messianic prophet speaking more often than any other prophet of the coming Messiah.

In the vision recorded in the sixth chapter Isaiah receives the disturbing and hard commission to go and tell his people: "Be ever hearing, but never understanding, be ever seeing, but never perceiving." These words have an ominous sound and are to be understood as such. Right at the beginning of his ministry, the prophet is told what kind of result he may expect. Worse, he is even to "make the heart of this people calloused", in other words to defeat the very purpose of his mission. Is not this an appalling contradiction? Again and again the Lord had called upon the people in His efforts to lead them in the right ways. Prophets came and went, but all to no avail. "The heart is deceitful above all things and beyond cure. Who can understand it?" (Jeremiah 17:9). At the time this vision was given, a battle was raging: the Assyrians were on the war-path, Samaria was doomed and the future of Judah hung in the balance. But the people thought that the calamity that overtook their land was due to an error in politics rather than to a failure in their relations to God. And so it seems that the only cure for wilful hardness of heart is to make this hardness absolute, so that punishment and guilt become one. No wonder the anguished cry is wrung from the prophet's throat: "For how long, O Lord?" He knows yet that this judgment is not God's last word, cannot be God's last word. Jonah also knew that the Lord is "a gracious and compassionate God, slow to anger and abounding in love, a God who repents from sending calamity" (Jonah 4:2; cf. Psalm103:8). And so Isaiah knew that this was not the end of the nation. Judgment, far from being absolute, is conditional. The prophet appealed in words designed to bring about insight and understanding: "Come, O house of Jacob, let us walk in the light" (2:5); "wash and make yourselves clean. Take your evil deeds out of My sight!" (1:16). God's anger does not by any means do away with His redeeming love:

"Surely God is my salvation;
I will trust and not be afraid;
The LORD, the LORD, is my strength and   my song;
He has become my salvation" (12:2).

And thus we find in the New Testament the words of Isaiah's commission quoted by our Lord in His ministry to the nation. He was to be the sin-offering (2 Corinthians 5:21; 1 Corinthians 15:3), taking upon Himself the punishment, so that the way to God is open once again (Hebr. 10:19-22).

There is yet another aspect, which helps us to see the non-finality of the hardening of Israel's heart. For the prophet calls his son Shear-jashub, i.e. "a remnant will return", return to the Mighty God (10:24). This remnant will be called "holy" (4:3). When an oak is cut down and the stump is left standing new branches may grow up. Just so the "holy seed" (6:13) means that through God's personal intervention – both selective and maintaining – the continuing existence of the nation is assured. In a reborn nation the work of sanctification will be achieved. The direct parallel in the New Testament is to be found when the Lord tells His disciples: "To you has been given to know the secrets of the Kingdom of God" (Matthew 13:11; Mark 4:11; Luke 8:10). Jeremias (*Parables*, p.16) says: "This is surely nothing less than a cry of exultation! God's gift is for the disciples." The disciples are the new nucleus of a remnant, constituting in a sense a holy seed from, and through which a new, obedient and holy nation of Israel will be built.

So we see that this word of the hardening of the heart, disturbing as it is, is not the only message the prophet proclaims. He is also the Prophet of the remnant.

In chapters 9 and 10 he is a herald of the coming Messiah. These two chapters are not restricted to his contemporaries, but reach beyond them to the ultimate redemption and ingathering of the exiles when "the earth will be full of the knowledge of the LORD as the waters cover the sea" (11:9). The LORD of the hardening of the heart is by no means God's last word. It is one of the singular works of the Lord in His dealing with the nation of Israel, and should be read within the larger framework of the drama of redemption. In 8:17 the prophet declares that he puts his trust in this very God, Who hardens the hearts and hides His face from the house of Jacob. Thus the hardening becomes an event which directs the prophet to the future. So, too, the Lord promises a day when whatever is hidden will be disclosed (Mark 4:22). We cannot but conclude, therefore, that the hardening of the heart is to be only temporary, and is, moreover, qualified by the creation of an obedient remnant.

As remarked before, the number of quotations from Isaiah looms large in the NT, but *how* are they used? Let us consider the first three verses of the gospel as reported by Mark:

> The beginning of the Gospel of Jesus the Messiah, the Son of God.
> Just as it stands written in Isaiah the prophet:
> "Look, I will send My messenger ahead of you,
> who will prepare your way,
> a voice of one calling in the desert,
> 'Prepare the way of the LORD,
> make straight paths for Him.'"

The first thing to be noticed is that the gospel, the "good news", "good tidings", stands in direct relation to the whole of God's revelation to His people in the past. The New Testament is not a breach with the OT, but a continuation and fulfilment of it (cf. Matthew 5:17). The OT quotations open with the prophetic *idou*, "look", to make the reader (or rather the hearer) attentive: "Mark well! It is God, Who is acting here!"

Under the name of Isaiah, Mark combines three OT passages given in the proper order of reading: first from the Torah (Exodus 23:20) and then the appropriate *haphtaroth*, or readings from the prophets, (Malachi 3:1 and Isaiah 40:3). Exodus fits Isaiah exactly;

it indicates the prospect of redemption; the new and ultimate redemption of which Isaiah speaks from chapter 40 onwards. Just as once against the Egyptians, the LORD will march out like a mighty warrior (42:13), and in this new exodus the LORD will again give His people to drink from the rock (48:21). But they will not leave in haste or go in flight, and the LORD Himself will be with them and guide them on the way (52:12). The second quotation is from Malachi and points to the appearance of John the Baptist. This link is laid again in Mark 9:11-13. It seems that Mark, after indicating the theme of the exodus, refers to the prophet Malachi regarding John the Baptist, and then to Isaiah regarding the Lord Jesus Christ. Should this be correct, *"Just as it stands written in Isaiah the prophet"* may be connected with *"the Gospel of Jesus the Messiah."* In that case the purport of the quotation is: this is the Gospel of Jesus the Messiah, that is to say the story of the redeeming exodus, just as Isaiah 40 onwards is a renewed reading of Exodus; read, therefore, from Isaiah 40:3 and you are reading the Gospel.

Now we can understand why Mark first speaks of the *Gospel of Jesus the Messiah* and a little later on of the gospel the Lord is proclaiming (1:14,15). Mark is writing the gospel of the Messiah in the same manner as Isaiah wrote it and so in the same manner as the Lord proclaimed it.

If we now look at the word *Gospel* itself, we shall find that Matthew Uses it 4 times, Acts only twice, but Mark as much as 8 times. Another 60 occurrences are in Paul. If we compare this with its cognate verb *euangelizoo*, "to preach the good news", we find that Mark never uses it, as against Luke 10 times, Acts 15 times and Paul 21 times. The Septuagint uses it 6 times in Isaiah: 40:9 (twice), 52:7 (twice) 60:6 and 61:1. Is it that Mark avoids the use of the verb, because Isaiah is and remains his evangelist? So much is certain that twice Isaiah explicitly gives the content of the good tidings: 40:9 "Here is your God!", and 52:7 "Your God reigns!" Can we wish for a better summary of the gospel according to Mark? As if to demonstrate that they have heard and understood, both Matthew and Luke each use one of the other two "gospel passages" from Isaiah; Matthew 2:11 quotes from Isaiah 60:6, and Luke 4:18-19 from Isaiah 61:1-2.

As if to stress this principle, Mark uses 7 times the word *gegraptai*, "it stands written: once to quote from Zachariah (Mark 14:27), three times from Isaiah (Mark 1:2; 7:6; 11:17). Twice it is written about the Son of Man (Mark 9:12; 14:21) and once about John the Baptist (Mark 9:13), continually referring to Isaiah.

All this does not mean that Isaiah alone should be read with Mark. The whole of the OT story remains vividly present, just as the book of Isaiah itself is a renewed reading of the previous Scriptures, with a view to the new exodus, the restoration of the Lord's reign and the re-election of His people. It does, however, amply demonstrate that the import of the Isaiah 6 passage should be read within the scope of the wider reaching message of the whole of Isaiah. Isaiah's mission also was to "strengthen the feeble hands, to steady the knees that give way" (Isaiah 35:3). The day will come when "the eyes of the blind will be opened, and the ears of the deaf unstopped" (Isaiah 35:5). "In that day the deaf will hear the words of the scroll, and out of the gloom and darkness the eyes of the blind will see" (Isaiah 29:18).

Happy eyes and ears

After this recalling of Isaiah's prophecy the Lord pronounces a blessing on the disciples, reported by Matthew (13:16) and Luke (20:23) in a slightly different form. Luke mentions only the eyes, possibly because in his context the emphasis is on the great deeds the disciples have seen. Matthew in his context of teaching gives the parallelism of both eyes and ears:

> happy are your eyes because they see,
> and your ears because they hear.

The word "blessed", as most versions have it here, is a translation of the Greek word *makarios*, and is well-known from the "Beatitudes" of the Sermon on the Mount. In its turn it is the equivalent of the Hebrew word *ashre*, which is the opening word of Psalm1. To distinguish this from the other word for "Blessed" it may seem better to use "happy", or, since it is a plural abstract noun in the original, "O, the happiness of". We have learned to realize the importance of the first occurrence of a word in the Bible. It's first occurrence, in this form, is in Deuteronomy 33:29. When Moses took his leave from the people, which he had led through the desert to the borders of the Promised Land, he said: "O the happiness of you, Israel! Who is like you, a people saved by the LORD? He is your shield, and helper and your glorious sword." This teaches us that the happiness of the nation is entirely dependent on God's election and salvation. This is confirmed when we consider some of the 26 occurrences of the word in the Book of Psalms. So in Psalm 33:12; "Happy is the nation whose God is the LORD, the people He chose for His inheritance". This happiness depends also on God's teaching (Psalm 94:12): "Happy is the man

You discipline, O Lord, the man You teach from Your law". And thus we begin to realize that this particular word is really sounding the praise of God's redemptive grace shown towards those He has chosen.

The second time we meet this word in the Scriptures is in relation to King Solomon (1 Kings 10:8; 2 Chronicles 9:7). After the queen of Sheba has seen all the wisdom and wealth of the king, she exclaims: "O the happiness of your men! O the happiness of your officials, who continually stand before you and hear your wisdom!" Notice these words "hear" and "wisdom". When the Lord Jesus Christ is speaking with His disciples, there is One greater than Solomon in their midst. Indeed, great is the happiness of the disciples when they are privileged to see His deeds and hear His words, for with them is the King of Kings and Lord of Lords Himself. He has been preaching that the Kingdom of the Heavens has drawn near and now initiates His disciples into some of its secrets.

The personification of "eyes" and "ears" is common in the Scriptures. In the Bible there is no dualism of soul and body. The words "eyes" and "ears" here stand for the whole person, even though the emphasis is on the acts of seeing and hearing as well as on what is seen and heard. The mighty works done by the Lord are the signs of the era of salvation, as the Lord made clear to the disciples of John the Baptist (Matthew 11:1-19; Luke 7:18-35). Obviously the need of true understanding of what is seen and heard is indicated in these words.

Earlier in the conversation the Lord had contrasted His circle of friends, including the Twelve, with the others from whom the secrets of the Kingdom of God were withheld. Now He contrasts them with the believers of bygone ages who with longing had looked forward to the days that the Kingdom of God would become manifest on this earth. Many prophets had spoken of it and many righteous men had believed that justice was to be established. What for those people had been an object of faith, hope and expectation, has now become reality and is for the disciples a matter of daily experience. Peter reminds us in his epistle (1:10-12) of the prophets who "searched intently", but were told "that they were not serving themselves…Even angels longed to look into these things." The thrust of the words is not just merely hearing the word of God in a general way, but hearing the proclamation that the age of redemption and salvation has come, that the reign of righteousness and justice has broken into the flow of human history.

The kingdom of the Heavens

At this point it seems proper to pause and consider the meaning of this expression "the Kingdom of God", or, as Matthew says, "the Kingdom of the Heavens". It falls outside the scope of this present study to deal with the bewildering array of different opinions on this subject, or even to discuss the manifold aspects described in the Scriptures. All we want to do is to trace a very rough outline for the reader to work out in further detail. It may be assumed as common knowledge that the Hebrew and Greek words do not primarily mean the territory over which a king rules, but rather the royal dignity, kingly authority, rule, sovereignty displayed and exercised by a "king". It may seem regrettable that the translators of the Authorized Version so often chose the word "kingdom" instead of "sovereignty", or "kingship", but this finds its origin in the usage of the word then. The Hebrew word was, quite correctly, also often translated "reign", and even as an adjective "royal" (royal wine, royal crown, etc.). In the Book of Esther (4:14), there is a very clear example which helps us to understand the primary meaning of the Hebrew word. The KJV has: "and who knoweth whether thou art come to the kingdom for such a time as this", but NIV translates: "And who knows but that you have come to royal dignity for such a time as this?"

It goes without saying that a king rules over a territory and the people living there. But we should not therefore take this derived and secondary meaning of the word "kingdom" and make it the primary meaning or even its only meaning in Scriptural usage.

The Bible opens with the majestic statement that God created the heavens and the earth and all that is in them. This means that God is the absolute Sovereign and that there is nothing above or beside Him to limit His supremacy. Psalm 50 expresses this very clearly: "The Mighty One, God, the LORD speaks and summons the earth from the rising of the sun to the place where it sets ... He summons the heavens above and the earth that He may judge His people," or Psalm 103:19; "The LORD has established His throne in the heavens, and His kingdom rules over all." "The LORD reigns, He is robed in majesty, the LORD is robed in majesty and is armed with strength" (Psalm 93:1). The destiny of the nations is in His hand: He orders the whole course of history in accordance with His plan (Isaiah 41:26; 45:1-6, etc.). The omnipotence of God is not in the first place an attribute of God telling of His perfection. It is the assurance that nothing can withstand His purpose. God's omnipotence is therefore closely connected with the purpose of human history. The Creator and Ruler of the world comprehends all things in one great plan, glimpses of which He has given to His servants the prophets. One of the fundamental verses for the OT conception of the kingdom of God is Zechariah 14:9: "The LORD will be King over the whole earth. On that day there will be one LORD, and His Name the only Name." This faith alone sustained the prophets and righteous people of the Old Testament through affliction and exile just as it has sustained the Jews these two millennia through catastrophe after catastrophe when experience and reason only seemed to lead into the deepest despair.

This cosmic dimension of God's sovereignty as Creator and King of the nations finds its particular expression in the grace bestowed upon the nation of Israel. The OT believers could look back to the redemption from Egypt, when His omnipotence took on a profound religious significance showing that it was directly related to His purpose in the world. Pharaoh had the arrogance to say: "who is the LORD that I should obey Him?" (Exodus 5:2). But Moses was fully confident and sang: "The LORD will reign for ever and ever (Exodus 15:18).

Out of all the nations of the earth the LORD God chose Israel, the smallest of them all (Deuteronomy 7:7; Amos 7:2,5; Isaiah 41:14) to be "for Him a kingdom of priests and a holy nation" (Exodus 19:3-8). Israel was to be the LORD's "precious possession", over which nobody else has any right and which has no relationship whatsoever to anybody else. This had, however, important consequences. Israel is not to exist for its own fame, its own glory; it is to become the symbol of the supreme rule of the Divine will on earth. God appoints Israel as His priestly ruler in relation to all the other nations, not in order that Israel should dominate the rest of the world in Gentile fashion, but that the nation over which God alone was King should serve the other nations as priest-king to bring them also into the obedience of the LORD.

When Israel failed to carry out their Divinely appointed task and as a whole became a failure, and the future looked dim and dismal, the prophets came to warn the nation and to admonish them to turn back to the God they had all but forgotten. The nation was to be punished for its idolatry and sins, but collapse and ruin are not the last word of God's plan. A new situation will emerge, in which idolatry, pride, wealth and militarism will be no more. Then Israel will bear the word of God to all nations, realizing al last the universal purpose of its Divine election.

One of the noblest expressions of the Israelite hope and expectation is given by Isaiah in his vision in chapter 2 of the days that God's rule will become manifest in the earth:

In the last days
the mountain of the LORD's temple will be established
as chief among the mountains;
it will be raised above the hills,
and all nations will stream to it.
Many peoples will come and say,
"Come, let us go up to the mountain of the LORD,
to the house of the God of Jacob.
He will teach us His ways,
so that we may walk in His paths."
The law will go out from Zion,
the word of the LORD from Jerusalem.
He will judge between the nations
and will settle disputes for many peoples.
They will beat their swords into pruning hooks.
Nation will not take up sword against nation,
nor will they train for war any more.

Here Zion is not depicted as the seat of the royal dynasty, not even as the capital of an Israelite empire, but as the center of God's universal reign. The religious aspect of the temple is ignored; it is here not the site of worship for all mankind (although we should not forget Isaiah 56:7), but the place from which justice and law go out to all men (compare 1 Kings 8:41-43). From His temple God will instruct ("judge" in the above translation) and arbitrate between nations, "so that they will beat their swords into plowshares and their spears into pruning hooks; nation shall not lift up sword against nation, neither shall they learn war any more". Because the lust for power and domination has come to an end, warfare will cease, and men will return to the simple life of farmers. Enduring peace will reign among nations.

The natural order also will be reformed: "The wolf will live with the lamb ... They will neither harm nor destroy on all My holy mountain, for the earth will be full of the knowledge of the LORD as the waters cover the sea" (Isaiah 11:6-9). Thus the enmity between animals and men that sprung up after the sin of Adam will disappear.

Isaiah is also the prophet who affirms that all men are to worship the one God at the end of the days. The destinies of Assyria, Moab, Damascus, Ethiopia and Egypt are all firmly linked to that of Israel, the people of God. The prophecy against Egypt closes with the blessing of the LORD Almighty; "Blessed be Egypt, My people; Assyria, My handiwork; and Israel, My inheritance" (Isaiah 19:15). This remarkable prophecy has no equal in the Scriptures. Nowhere else is the LORD represented as calling a foreign nation "My people".

In Jeremiah 10:7 the LORD is called "the King of the nations". The apparent difference between "I am the LORD, Almighty, the God of mankind" (Jeremiah 32:27) and "the LORD Almighty, the God of Israel" (Jeremiah 32:15) is to be explained by the double relation of God to the world in general, and to Israel in particular. He is the LORD of all nations while His Name is especially attached to Israel.

When the Lord taught His disciples to pray: "Thy Kingdom come", He taught them to pray that God's rule might become manifest on this earth. And He continued: "*Thy will be done* on earth as it is done in heaven". The disciples were to pray that God's sovereignty and power might become manifest, that every enemy of His Divine rule be put to naught, that God alone might be King over all the affairs of mankind.

All too often it is forgotten or ignored that the Lord did not proclaim the nearness of the kingdom of the Heavens in a vacuum. The nation of Israel was subject to the Roman empire. Relations between the Jews and their foreign rulers were tense and strained. In 6 A.D. revolt had broken out under Judas the Galilean, and was to flare up again in 40 A.D., when Caligula defiled the Temple. Trouble was constantly brewing, and minor tragedies took place (Luke 13:1-3). This tense political situation made it the right moment for God to act. "Man's extremity is God's opportunity", "when the time had fully come, God sent His son" (Galatians 4:4). The Lord came to herald that the hour of promise had at last struck and that through Him the age of glorious blessedness foretold and longed for throughout past ages was at last to begin (Mark 1:15); Luke 4:19). If Israel was to fulfil its destiny now was the time. His coming was the great intervention of God, His proclamation of the Kingdom was the loving offer of God Himself.

The necessary condition for entering the Kingdom of the Heaven is given in the call to repentance. Repentance (*metanoia*) is not just sorrow for past sins, but goes much deeper. It means a radical turning around and re-thinking to come into a new allegiance to God and a real acceptance of the new way of life. A good paraphrase of the Lord's summons might be "The time has fully come for God's rule to be established on earth – turn right about face and make His thoughts and ways your own – believe this good news and act upon it, and this glorious thing will come to pass" (R. Dunkerley, *The Hope of Jesus*, page 54). That great blessings were speedily possible may be deduced from the Lord's own words in Matthew 9:37 and Luke 10:2: "The harvest is indeed plentiful, but the workers are few. Ask the Lord of the harvest, therefore, to send out workers into His harvest field". What might have been the result if the nation had responded can only be a matter of speculation. The longings of the Old Testament prophets were admirably summed up in the angel's song of peace and goodwill. And Jerusalem might have become at that time the center of missionary light to the world. "And all mankind would have seen God's salvation" (Luke 3:6). But as things turned out, Jerusalem "did not recognize the time of God's coming to them" (Luke 19:44).

After the Lord's death and resurrection, the Apostles take up the call of repentance once more, Acts 2:38 and 3:19,20. Peter tells the men of Israel: "Repent ... that times of refreshing may come from the Lord, and that He may send the Christ ..., who is to sit at His right hand until all His enemies are made a footstool for His feet (Acts 2:34,35).

The Parable of the Sower forms a beautiful illustration of the expectation of the Lord Himself at the moment of telling; even though some seed will be lost, by far the greatest part of it is expected to render an abundant harvest.

There are, of course, many more aspects of the Kingdom of the Heavens with which we cannot deal in the scope of this study, yet we may point in passing to Matthew 19, where we find several synonyms: eternal life (16), life (17), the Kingdom of the Heavens (23), the Kingdom of God (24), to be saved (25). Probably the best definition is the one offered by G.E. Ladd in *The Gospel of the Kingdom,* page 107: "The Kingdom of God in the New Testament is the redemptive work of God active in history for the defeat of His enemies, bringing to men the blessings of the divine reign". So much is certain: during the Lord's ministry there was a real possibility of God's rule coming on earth, and, on the basis of His victory over sin and death, this was once more a real possibility during the Acts period. Now with these thoughts about the

Kingdom in mind, we shall turn back to the Parable of the Sower, to try and understand our Lord's explanation to His disciples.

The explanation of the Parable

Mark lays much stress on the importance of this parable, opening the Lord's interpretation of it with this question: "If you do not understand (*oida*) this parable how will you be able to grasp (*ginosko*) the nature of any of the parables?" Mark very nicely makes use of two different words. The paraphrase given above tries to bring this out more clearly in English. Apparently, Mark wants to bring it home to his readers that this parable is the point of departure for all the other parables which the Lord taught later. Mark then continues: "The sower sows the word". This is the one parable in which no explanation is given for the sower. This should make us listen all the more intently, since it seemed superfluous to the Lord to say more on this point. The seed is explained by Luke as the word (*logos*) of God, or, as Matthew says: the *logos* of the Kingdom.

It is not revealed who is the sower and he plays no further part in the interpretation. The teaching of the Lord Jesus Christ is designated by Luke as "the word of God" (5:1), practically implying that the "sower" is none other than the Lord Himself. In Luke 8:21 and 11:28 it says that it is essential not only to hear the word of God, but also to obey it and to make it work in one's life. "At the moment when He was telling the parable, Christ was sowing the seed of the word, and thus, by telling the parable, He was actually exemplifying it" (Cole, *Mark*, p. 92).

In Acts, Luke uses this same phrase, "the word of God', for the proclamation of the Apostles, leaving the way open to apply the image of "the sower" to them as well. The Apostles' teaching is not merely the words of men (1 Thessalonians 2:13), it is the imperishable seed of which men have been born again (1 Peter 1:23).

Although the seed is "the word of God", the people hearing the message are identified with it, or rather with the plants that grow from the seed. This image of the sower and his sowing is known from the prophets. "The days are coming", declare the LORD, "that I will sow the house of Israel and the house of Judah with the seed of men and the seed of animals" (Jeremiah 31:27). This is followed by the prophecy of the new covenant the LORD will conclude with Israel and Judah. Hosea, too, pictures the restoration of Israel under the image of sowing (2:21-23). Therefore, this imagery of sowing in the Old Testament requires a Messianic application. God Himself is the sower. His redemptive work in Israel is compared to the going out of the sower. In Israel God had experienced failure upon failure. It seemed as if He had sown on barren soil. Now the parable of the Lord Jesus Christ is a parable of contrast. Over against the earlier activity of the sower He tells of the eventual success. This is God acting in sovereign graciousness toward men.

In the ministry of Jesus, God's action in history has come into a new and decisive stage. Now at last it will bear fruit in Israel. His redemptive rule has invaded the world of men and its triumph is certain! This will be the miracle of the abundant harvest in the Kingdom. "Then the land will yield its harvest, and God, our God, will bless us" (Psalm 67:6).

Yet Divine Love cannot coerce, it can only offer and plead and persuade and suffer. For the Word of the Kingdom to bear fruit, it is necessary that there is willingness to accept it. As it is there are some people who hear the message but do not seem to "treasure" up the words in their hearts as Mary did. People may attend church and Gospel meetings. They hear the words, seem favorably impressed, often speak with appreciation of what they heard, but only a little later on there are those birds again and the seed is snatched away. Of course, this is figurative language. But is not this the dark and terrible puzzle in human life, that words of such vital importance just seem to disappear into thin air? It is the dark enigma of the not-good earth, and who can tell whether it is a person's own fault or just their inability? Here Scripture does not answer the problem. "The sole point made in the parable is that men's hearts do in fact so vary, and that this variation governs their response" (Cole, *Mark*; p.93). Exactly for this reason the admonition is sounded: "Let the wicked forsake his way and the evil man his *thoughts*" (Isaiah 55:7).

God gives food and fertile seed, but the message should not be allowed to fall flat, but should be heard with faith. To stress this point Luke adds in 8:12 and 13 "believe", directing our attention to the initial proclamation of the Lord: "Repent and believe!" (Mark 1:15). This is the same as "hears My words and puts them into practice" (Luke 6:47). We can almost feel the pain with which the Lord utters these words: "that they may not (begin to, aorist participle) believe and be saved", for on their faith in Him hinges both physical healing for Israel and their spiritual salvation.

Although the type of soil is the object of interest, Luke's use of the masculine "those along the path" may refer, as plainly stated by Matthew and Mark, to the persons represented by the seeds. Luke has already said, though, that the seed is the word of God. This may seem odd at first sight, but if we want to come to a proper understanding of this parable, we shall have to allow this two-fold application. Basically, it is the seed sown "in them" (Mark), "in his heart" (Matthew) and taken "from their hearts" (Luke), for the heart is the seat of thinking in Scripture, "it is the wellspring of life" (Proverbs 4:23). On the other hand, the Lord is said "to sow the land" with people, Jeremiah 31:27, Hosea 2:23; Zechariah 10:9. So the change-over from seed to people is not quite so unexpected as is sometimes thought.

As for the seed that falls into the rocky places, it represents those people who receive with joy the word of the Good News that the Kingdom has drawn near. When, however, further words seem to go against the grain, those people cannot bear them any longer: may even be filled with anger like the people of Nazareth (Luke 4:14-28). Some teaching of the Lord may be difficult to understand, with the result (John 6:60-66) that many of the disciples turn back and no longer follow Him. This is what is meant by Luke's expression "they fall away". The Greek verb is the same as that used in Luke 2:37, where we are told that Anna did not "depart from" the temple, but spent her time there in religious devotions. Matthew And Mark use the verb derived from the noun *skandalon*, stumbling block, a stone or obstacle in the way over which one can trip and fall. This expression is often used of the Lord Jesus Christ in the New Testament. Right at the beginning Simeon said, "This child is destined to cause the falling and rising of many in Israel, and to be a sign that will be spoken against" (Luke 2:34). He still remains for many "a stone that causes men to stumble and a rock that makes them fall" (1 Peter 2:8).

The cause of this failure is that these people have "no root in themselves" which, of course, means that there is no developed root system. It does not speak of the people themselves, but rather of their rooting in the soil. It is not the strength of the root which the Lord has in mind, but its function in supplying "moisture" for the plant.

The new life God gives does not merely exist in "growing up" and heavenward in praise and thanksgiving, it is also "growing down"; "So then, just as you received Christ Jesus as Lord, continue to live in Him, rooted and built up in Him" (Colossians 2:7). Compare also Ephesians 3:17 and 18. How can we develop a "root system"? Psalm 1 shows the way unequivocally: living by every word that goes out from the Lord. For this reason the Apostle Paul exhorted the Colossians (Colossians 3:16): "Let the word of Christ dwell in you richly".

Then we have the third type of sowing. Those people who hear the word and seem to show a lot of promise, but apparently have not enough single-mindedness of purpose. In this life there are so many beautiful things to be enjoyed. But even though the good things in life are by no means to be despised, we should be fully aware of the fact that "the kingdom of God is not a matter of eating and drinking, but of righteousness, peace and joy in the Holy Spirit" (Romans 14:17). There is nothing wrong with the seed, it has a large potential for spiritual advance, but we should not be filling our lives with so many things that there is no room left for spiritual fruit.

There are also many worries, anxieties and cares in this life. In another context the Lord Jesus Christ warns His disciples to be careful lest their hearts are weighed down with the anxieties of life (cf. Luke 21:34). King David knew the answer already: "Cast your care on the Lord and He will sustain you" (Psalm 55:22) and the Apostle Peter repeats this many centuries later: "Cast all your anxiety on Him because He cares for you" (1 Peter 5:7). To become entangled in the worries of this life is as sinful as living in drunkenness. The thistles and thorns will grow faster than the seed.

When speaking of wealth, our thoughts tend to turn to the rich who live in luxury. We may then think of that rich young ruler who turned away from the Lord sorrowfully (Matthew 19:16-30) and par.). But material abundance and riches do not choke a person all at once. Like the weeds in the parable they take time to grow up, and often only slowly strangle the spiritual life within. We often find that a Christian man settles on a plateau in middle life – he is a good father, successful in business, "a good man in the meetings" – but he leaves real spiritual development until his retirement. And then he finds he no longer has the drive he used to. He is another candidate for those people in their seventies and eighties who find life nothing but a burden.

In the telling of the parable Mark gives the additional note: "and they did not bear fruit" (4:7). Do we not hear the Lord heave a sigh of sadness and sorrow? This parable is one of hearing. Obeying and, therefore, doing is implicit in hearing. No doubt you have heard a father or mother say to a disobedient child: "Now did you hear me? Then do as I told you". In Greek "to obey" is a composite verb of "to hear", and in Hebrew both are the same verb, *shamah*. In several modern languages these two verbs are formed from the same stem, "to hear", thus throwing into relief the close relation between the two actions. If we are only hearing, without giving attention and then putting into practice, we remain "unfruitful". In the explanation of the parable Luke has "they do not bear fruit to maturity" (8:14).

A popular view of conversion sees it as a once-in-a-lifetime experience. If that is the way we feel about it, it is apt to leave our worldly values untouched. Milk is an excellent food for newborn babies (1 Peter 2:2) and we should crave the pure spiritual milk so that we may thrive on it to our soul's health (NEB). But Paul's complaint was that many Christians needed to be taught the ABCs of God's word all over again (Hebrews 5:12). They kept feeding on baby milk instead of being weaned and getting accustomed to take solid food, cf. also 1 Corinthians 3:1-4. Land that drinks in the rain often falling on it and that produces a crop useful to those for whom it is farmed receives the blessing of God. But land that produces thorns and thistles is worthless." (Hebrews. 6:7,8). Therefore, let us go on to maturity.

And that is exactly what is shown in the fourth type of sowing. For those people of the good soil Mark uses the pronoun *ekeinoi* in verse 20. This should indeed not be translated in the same way as the *houtoi* in verses 15,16,18. It is most definitely not the same. If scripture uses a different word we should be attentive and consider carefully how we listen and what we hear. One of the many usages of the pronoun *ekeinos* is that it can be used to place one thing over against another thing, to differentiate "this" from "that". It can also be used to bring the thing or person indicated into special prominence. In consonance with the parable itself Mark emphasizes once again (cf. page 7) that most of the seed is going to produce fruit and to yield an abundant crop. The "and" with which verse 20 opens may almost have the meaning of "but", giving even more emphasis to the fact that this is what the entire parable has been leading up to.

All these other people not only heard, but also treasured up what they heard in a noble and good heart. They are not distracted like Martha with all the preparations that have to be made. The Lord kindly told her to stop fretting and fussing about so many things, and added that "only one thing is necessary. The part that Mary has chosen is best, and it shall not be taken away from her" (Luke 10:40-42).

Luke ends on the telling note that this crop was produced "by their perseverance", "by standing firm you will gain life" (Luke 21:19). The "good soil", of course, is the well cultivated ordinary field of good quality. It is the opened heart that sits at the master's feet and stays there listening to what He says. Faith is brought to a more mature level by a correct way of teaching. It wants to get hold of something and thus it is essential that a person understands. Just reading the Bible without taking in its meaning and thought, is of no great use. Nor does it do much good to print Bible texts and memorize them without distinguishing by whom, to whom and in what context they were spoken. Knowledge of these things is necessary to understand correctly what the Scripture means. Only by understanding can we relate to God's thoughts. The result is that we can act upon it and put it into practice. This cannot be achieved apart from the work of the Holy Spirit. The Lord promised His disciples that He would send them the Holy Spirit, "and He will guide you into all truth" (John 16:13). In our present dispensation and under different circumstances this holds as well. "Continue to work out your salvation with fear and trembling, for it is God who works in you, inspiring both the will and the deed, for His own chosen purpose" (Philippians 2:12,13).

A popular view is that bearing fruit means engaging in evangelizing or missionary activity. These two things then tend to become synonymous. More work done in the service of the Lord, more souls won for Him, is bearing more fruit. But at harvest time the farmer does not want a large field of small plants, he wants a ripe harvest. That does not in the least alter the fact that each and every Christian loves to be a witness to his Lord and to win souls for Him. In secular life he certainly will not be the last to give help to his neighbor or to render charity. But that is not what this parable speaks of. It is the person's spiritual maturity that stands in the foreground here.

When a person has opened ears and seeing eyes, he receives the Word of God as seed that takes root in the soil of his life and then grows. On that condition alone he is able to absorb "moisture" so as not to wither. Let us always keep in mind the purpose of God: "So that the man who belongs to God may be efficient and thoroughly equipped (combining NEB with NIV) for good work of every kind" (2 Timothy 3:17). And we have the statement of the Lord: "so shall the word which comes from My mouth prevail; It shall not return to Me fruitless, but shall accomplish what I desire and achieve the purpose for which I sent it" (Isaiah 55:11). When the Lord closes this parable by showing that the rich and fruitful life is a result of the word of God, it goes far to prove that a sound and ripe harvest is not only what the heavenly Father desires, but also that He wants to see His purpose achieved.

And so the first parable ends on a note of triumph. The majority of people hear the word with a noble and good heart, accept it, understand it, retain it and produce an abundant crop by their perseverance. They are the ones who form the good soil for the "gospel of the glory of Christ", so that sons of the kingdom are not just 25% of the seed sown. Although some seed was lost, most of it resulted in an unheard of crop.

Further observations

After John the Baptist was put into prison, the Lord Jesus Christ began His public ministry, proclaiming: "The time has fully come. The Kingdom of God is near. Repent and believe the good news!" (Mark 1:15).

But what "time" is this and what does it mean by the time has fully come? The Greek language has different words for "time". The Lord did not use the word *chronos*, indicating the general flow of time, the totality of moments and events. He used the word *kairos*, the word which speaks of a very definite moment, one especially designated by God. *Kairos* characterizes a critical situation, a special point of time which demands action. In the Greek version of the Old Testament the phrase "at that time" directs attention to God's redeeming intervention in the history of the nation, especially to the time of Moses and the exodus from Egypt. Then the nation experienced a series of manifestations of the divine sovereignty. In the prophets this phrase took on a future reference, and look forward to that precious moment when God has again to intervene in human affairs to bring about redemption and salvation not only for the nation but even for all the people. Now the Lord proclaims that this long-awaited moment has come, God's sovereignty is already being manifested here and now.

The kingdom of God is near. "Is near" sounds a bit weak; the Greek verb also has the meaning "has arrived", "is present". On a later occasion the Lord said: "But if it is by the Spirit of God that I drive out demons, then be sure the kingdom of God has already come upon you" (Matthew 12:28 NEB). A modern commentator gave this paraphrase: "The sovereignty of God brought near, in the sense of being arrived, corresponds to Jesus' concept of the kingdom of God as a powerful, dynamic event, in which God universally sets up His rule of salvation; God's sovereignty breaks in".

Just as John before Him, the Lord adds the summons: "Repent and believe the good news". "To repent" is not a very felicitous translation of the original. It does not mean "to regret", "to see the error of one's way". The Greek word represents the Hebrew word for "to turn", "to return (to God)." It is a compound of *nous*, implying that the will and the thought are involved. It is neither a purely outward act of turning, nor a merely intellectual change of ideas. It is rather the decision of the whole man to turn around, a change in thinking as well as behavior is stressed. It was not for nothing that John demanded: "Prove that you changed your life and thought by producing fruit in keeping with this reversal" (Matthew 3:8; Luke 3:8).

It should be kept in mind that life under Roman rule was no joke. The devout and faithful were earnestly waiting for the kingdom of God (Joseph of Arimathea, Mark 15:43), the consolation of Israel (Simeon, Luke 2:24, cf: Isaiah 40). Some, however, wanted to fight the Roman might with the sword. The majority of the people chafed and submitted. The New Testament does not say much about the political situation. How bad things could be is hinted at in Luke 13:1-3, where the Lord emphasized His demand for a radical change. He warned the people that unless they turned about and gave unstinted allegiance to the rule of God as represented by Him, they would all of them come to the same end. What exactly did the Lord want? "Love your enemies, bless those who curse you, do good to those who hate you, and pray for them who persecute you and for those who treat you spitefully" (Matthew 5:44). Not an easy way of life, and especially not for the Israelite of that time.

The struggle with Rome meant death. The Lord did not preach resistance to Rome, but neither did He teach that it is expedient to submit, with hatred in one's heart. No, He gave quite a different solution to the problem. The only remedy to avert war and destruction would be for the Jews to rise to an understanding of their true vocation, the vocation of showing mercy to the world that was pressing in all round them, of giving freely their knowledge of God for the benefit of humanity rather than sullenly insisting on religious privileges as an exclusive possession. No wonder He wept on the day of His triumphal entry into Jerusalem, and said: "If you had only known on this great day what would bring you peace (or: the way that leads to peace, NEB) ... they will not leave you one stone standing on another because you did not recognize the time of God's coming to you" (Luke 19:41-44). KJV has here: "time of thy visitation". This last word refers to divine intervention for the purpose of bringing salvation and blessing. It forms an easy link to Luke 1:68; "Praise be to the LORD, the God of Israel, because He has come (KJV He has visited) and has redeemed His people"; and Luke 1:78,79; "because of the tender mercy of our God, by which the rising sun will come to us (KJV visit us) from heaven ... to guide our feet into the path of peace."

Much has been made of the failure of the people to recognize the authority of the Lord Jesus Christ and therefore to submit to His demands. Subsequent history has not failed to give prominence to the fact that the kingdom was not consummated in our Lord's time. But that should not blind our eyes to the other side of the picture. In spite of all the opposition and ill-will, there was a great measure of success. True, the Lord's earthly ministry tended in His death. But this resulted in, and led to, His great triumph over death and the devil. So was His ministry a failure? Was God's purpose frustrated?

John the Baptist, as the forerunner of the Lord Jesus Christ, was largely accepted by the people of Israel then living in the land; "People went out to him from Jerusalem and all Judea and the whole region of the Jordan", (Matthew 3:5; Mark 1:5). His short ministry produced a state of mind where God's truth was credible to all those many people who heard it.

When the Lord Jesus Christ came, He went throughout Galilee, teaching in their synagogues and proclaiming the good news of the Kingdom. "Large crowds from Galilee, the Decapolis, Jerusalem, Judea and the region across the Jordan followed Him" (Matthew 4:23-25). If ever any man on earth enjoyed a successful ministry, so far as public response is concerned, it was the Lord Jesus Christ. The sight of the multitudes moved Him to pity; they were like sheep without a shepherd, harassed and helpless. Yet He said to His disciples: "The harvest is plentiful, but the workers are few" (Matthew 9:37, Luke 10:2). And He was not referring to some distant future: "Do you not say, "Four months and then the harvest"? I tell you, open your eyes and look at the fields! They are ripe for harvest" (John 4:35). The multitudes continued to follow Him and to receive His blessings (Matthew 19:2; 20:29), even up to His entrance into Jerusalem. And when the opposing leaders determined to kill Him, they feared the multitude (Matthew 21:46).

When we come to the Acts period, we find that the number of those who believed increased at a tremendous pace. On the day of Pentecost 3000 souls were added in the very city in which the Lord Jesus had been condemned to death. The second massage of Peter had further astonishing results (Acts 4:4). Twenty-five years later, Paul was told: "you see, brother, how many tens of thousands of Jews have believed, all of them staunch upholders of the law" (Acts 21:20_. The word "thousands" which most versions have here, is a mistranslation of the Greek word "*myriad*", which means ten thousand. If we accept the different scholarly estimates that the resident population of Jerusalem at that time may have been somewhere between 30,000 and 50,000, it is easy to see that most of the people living in Jerusalem and its immediate surroundings had become converts to the Christian faith.

In spite of all this, the kingdom of God was not consummated. Another dispensation was introduced and the prophetic promises to Israel were suspended. Instead of acting in government, God is now acting in grace. As a result, this parable of the sower has become prophecy. Although during the Acts period a firstfruits was seen, we are still awaiting the full realization of it. Once this present dispensation has run its full course in God's eyes, He will return His Salvation to the people of Israel, gather them out of the nations, and by sending the full blessing of the Holy Spirit, work at the specific Kingdom purposes which have been held in abeyance for almost two thousand years now.

Conclusions

The Jewish expectation of the Messiah was that he was to appear in outward glory to subdue God's enemies and then to establish the kingdom by a great display of power. (This was certainly not a complete misunderstanding of what the prophets of the OT had said about the coming intervention of God). When God considered the time ripe for the sending of His Son, He came as the lowly suffering One.

His messenger had gone before him and had prepared the people. And now the Messiah Himself appeared. The divine sovereignty to bring deliverance was at work in Christ. His works witnessed to that. He began to proclaim the Kingdom. For that purpose He had come into the world. But He did not come in terms of earthquake, wind and fire. He came in the sound of gentle stillness, as a low murmuring sound, in a gentle whisper.

In His parables, the Lord began to show different aspects of the Kingdom, so as to teach the people in general, and His disciples in particular, what was to be the actual course of the Kingdom. The parable of the sower sets the theme for this teaching.

John the Baptist had prepared the field for the Sower. The seed is of divine origin. It will do the work it is meant to do. But there may be hindrances to this work. God does not force the people against their will. He allows them, as it were, their own dignity. This is very explicitly said by the Lord Himself: "How often have I longed to gather you children together…but you were not willing" (Matthew 23:37. Luke 31:34). The kingdom of God is God's dynamic activity through and in His Son. Even though a certain amount of seed was to all appearances wasted, most of it was to produce abundant fruit.

This parable also shows the human responsibility. True, "a man can receive only what is given him from heaven" (John 3:27), but "a noble and good heart is of vital importance not only to hear the word, but also to retain and understand it. In this parable the Lord shows divine responsibility coming alongside human responsibility. Redemption becomes impossible for those who reject His call.

One question, however, remains open at this point. In this parable the final end of history is not in sight. It does not proceed beyond the stage of fruit-bearing. Historically speaking we have not even seen that harvest in full. The Acts period bore rich promises. The divine sovereignty that delivers and transforms humanity in the entirety of its relations has manifestly not come to pass. "The night is almost over; the day is almost here" (see Romans 13:12). But the day has not come so far. God had another purpose that intervened. And thus the final issue of the parable of the sower seems to turn into a prophecy of what is still to be expected, when God shall have restored the nation of Israel and shall have rebuilt the fallen tent of David, all the world will see that full and abundant harvest in the consummation of the age.

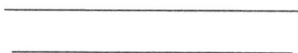

More on Parables

The Purpose of Parables
By Michael Penny

The Purpose
of Parables

So why did Christ start teaching in Parables? He had not done so for the first part of his ministry ... so why did He start? That is what the disciples wanted to know and His answer was ...

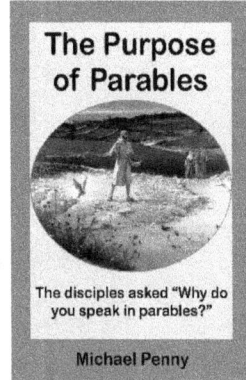

The disciples asked "Why do you speak in parables?"

Michael Penny

"Because the knowledge of the secrets of the kingdom of heaven has been given to you, but not to them."

- So who were the 'you' and who were the 'them'?
- And how do parables reveal secrets to the 'you' but conceal the meaning from the 'them'?

Further details of the above, and the books on the next pages, can be seen on **www.obt.org.uk**

They can be ordered from that website and from

The Open Bible Trust
Fordland Mount, Upper Basildon,
Reading, RG8 8LU, UK.

They are also available as eBooks from Amazon and Apple, and as paperbacks from Amazon.

More on Matthew

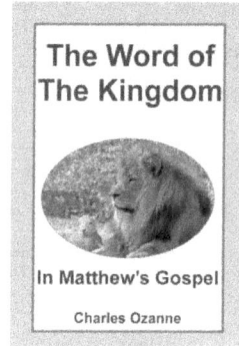

The Word of the Kingdom in Matthew's Gospel

By Charles Ozanne

In this publication Charles Ozanne sheds new light on many well know and familiar passages of Matthew's Gospel in general and the Kingdom in particular.

The Sermon on the Mount, the Lord's prayer, the Parables of Chapter 13, the Prophecy of chapter 24 and the Great Commission, with which the Gospel ends, are all given due consideration.

Signs of the Second Coming (Matthew 24)

Michael Penny

Open Bible Trust conferences held in at Nottingham, Somerset, and Kent dealt with the subject of The Return of Christ. Some of the issues dealt with were:-

- "When will he return?",
- "Can we know the date?", and
- "What events precede his coming?"

The studies given at those conferences provoked many questions, and what follows is based upon those studies and the issues raised by those questions.

More on The Gospels

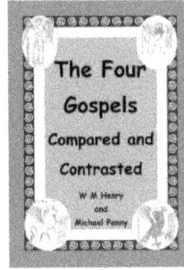

Christ' New Commandment by Bryan Conway
Becoming Born Again by Ken Evans
Was John the Baptist Elijah? by Michael Penny
The Four Gospels: Compared and Contrasted by W M Henry
and Michael Penny

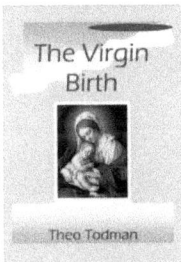

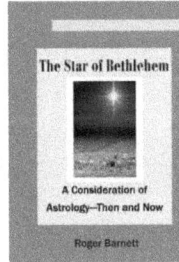

The Virgin Birth by Theo Todman
The Signs in John's Gospel by W M Henry
The Temptations of the Lord by Theo Todman
The Star of Bethlehem by Roger Barnett

For more information on these titles please visit
www.obt.org.uk

Free Magazine

For a free sample of
the Open Bible Trust's magazine Search,
please email

admin@obt.org.uk

or visit

www.obt.org.uk/search

About the author

Nico Baalbergen was born in 1924 in Haarlem near Amsterdam in the Netherlands. He read language and literature at the University of Utrecht and went to live in New Zealand from 1950 to 1958, before returning to the Netherlands. He then read theology at the University of Utrecht after which he worked in Christian Radio and the teaching profession where he taught religious education.

About this book

The Parable of the Sower

During His time on earth, the Lord Jesus Christ taught many things by way of *parables*, outstanding among them is *The Parable of the Sower*. As a parable it stands on its own and seems to be a key to understanding all other parable, for Christ insisted, "You do not understand this parable? How them are you able to understand any parable?" (Mark 4:13).

The author gives a thorough and thought-provoking treatment of *The Parable of the Sower,* linking it very much to the kingdom of God which he emphasizes as 'then kingdom of **God**'. Thus, neither the parable nor the kingdom can be understood apart from God's sovereignty intervening in the affairs of man … for no amount of human effort will bring about **His** kingdom.

Publications of The Open Bible Trust must be in accordance with its evangelical, fundamental and dispensational basis. However, beyond this minimum, writers are free to express whatever beliefs they may have as their own understanding, provided that the aim in so doing is to further the object of The Open Bible Trust. A copy of the doctrinal basis is available at

www.obt.org.uk/doctrinal-basis

or from:

THE OPEN BIBLE TRUST
Fordland Mount, Upper Basildon,
Reading, RG8 8LU, GB